Poop Poems
by
T.R. Swerdlow

A book for those who look.

I just took a hot-headed stallion of a dump that kicked the barn door open and ran away for good.

My asshole must be
playing an Indian flute
because there's a big
brown snake craning
its neck in the toilet.

I just took a giant
lucky horseshoe of a
poo that has me thinking
think I should go by a
lottery ticket.

Some shredded
documents just flew
out of my ass,
evidence of a crime I don't
remember committing.

I may have eaten an
accordion because I
just took a three
verse hookless shit
that will only play on
Mexican radio.

I just took a middle linebacker of a shit. It shot the gap and tackled the water for a five-yard loss.

The tanker of my ass
just had an oil spill
and birds with sticky
wings are flailing in the
bowl.

I just dropped a stinky ripe
rigatoni shit that was
almost as satisfying as
the meal itself.

I just parted ways with
a three-chapter
gut clearer that
started with a
heavy gold bar and
ended like a sparrow
that's been blasted
with a shotgun.

If you glanced at what
just came out of my ass
you'd think I ate the
front lawn yesterday.

I just folded a pair of
brown slacks into a
drawer at the second-
floor shitter at the TJ
Maxx in Santa Monica.

Don't look now but a 3-pound cow shit just
      shipwrecked itself in
         my toilet like a
         battered brown
           freighter.

I just gave birth to an
exploding cigar of a
dump, and the
safety match to light it.

A thief of a dook
just snuck out of my ass,
quiet as a mouse
and pockets heavy
with silver.

I just had a bowel movement three different ways, and the chef came out to the table and asked me if I enjoyed it.

A set of Russian nesting dolls
    has set up shop
  in the sweet blue tile
 confines of my home
     court crapper.

I just took a firm
frozen custard of a shit,
that would put mister softee
in a jealous tizzy.

I just got some distance from a
Coffee-powered zinger
and I may just dance the cha cha
before I wipe.

A family of eels just
dove out of my ass and
were happy to be back
in the water and the
hell away from me.

I just scattered some
noxious scraps in the
death pond to tepid
applause from an
expectant but
disappointed crowd.

A mumbling shit
just fell out of my ass
that couldn't
complete a sentence.

I just said farewell
to an old shoe of a shit,
the laces frayed and a
hole in the toe.

I just published an
Upanishad of a poop
that smelled of cumin
and spanned across centuries
and I may need the four hands
of Shiva to wipe.

I just took a dump
that looked like Chinese
handcuffs, but I
wouldn't want to stick
my fingers in.

A skateboard ramp just
fell out of my tush, the
odor reminiscent of
Thanksgiving and
oddly reassuring.

I just wrote a brown
short story torn from
the headlines.

Someone must be up my ass with a pail
because I just shat a sandcastle.

Back at Noah's public crapper
and somehow an
old rotten log
torn apart by an
M80 has fallen
out of my hiney.

A soft meteor
just flew out of my derriere
and into a porcelain orbit.

I just dropped a few
Vietnamese sampans
out of my butt
and now they're floating in the
gulf of Tonkin.

I just let go of something
that looks like one sad eel looking
for a school of
eels.

I just let go of an
unexpected burden at
the Pali hotel and
altered the
aromatherapy of the
universe.

Last night it was
macaroni and cheese
this morning it's something
you could insulate
your attic with.

I just put down a load at
the old hotel that
would work as a
counterweight for an
elevator.

A breaching
brown whale of a shit
Was just spotted off starboard
And I didn't have my binoculars.

I just sploshed some suds mud all over the artisan coffee shop shitter out in Santa Monica.

I just took the kind of
shit beggars take in
Mumbai.

I just took a dump that sounded like it dropped from fifty feet and I'm feeling pretty damn good about myself.

A good sized shipping hook just dropped out of my ass but I feel like it's only the tip of the iceberg.

I just took a shit in the
Korean hotel formed
by a thousand years of
wind and rain.

Some dark matter
just fled my backside
that can only be ordered "off the menu".

I just let go of a lot of childhood trauma, a few shredded truck tires and a little league banquet meal from 1973.

T.R. Swerdlow goes in Los Angeles.

www.ingramcontent.com/pod-product-compliance
Ingram Content Group UK Ltd.
Pitfield, Milton Keynes, MK11 3LW, UK
UKHW022240230426
12048UKWH00018BA/1383